OUTLINES ON THE NEW TESTAMENT

C. W. Keiningham

BAKER BOOK HOUSE
Grand Rapids, Michigan 49516

a division of Baker Book House Company
P.O. Box 6287, Grand Rapids, MI 49516-6287

ISBN: 0-8010-5279-3

Sixth printing, January 1999

Printed in the United States of America

For information about academic books, resources for Christian leaders, and all new releases available from Baker Book House, visit our web site:
http://www.bakerbooks.com/

Contents

1

The Church Victorious

Matthew 16:13–19

Various interpretations of "upon this rock" are:

The person of Simon Peter.
The person of Jesus himself.
Professions like Simon Peter's.

I. **The Church's Advantage.**
   A. We have a great God—the God of Moses, Elijah, Daniel, and so forth.
   B. We have a great Savior (Heb. 7:25).
   C. We have a great high priest (Heb. 4:14; 7:25).
   D. We have a great Bill of Rights (Bible).
      1. It guarantees God's presence (Matt. 28:20).
      2. It guarantees God's power (Matt. 28:18).
   E. We have a great helper (Acts 1:8).
   F. We have a unique privilege—freedom in Christ.
   G. We have a great opportunity (Rev. 3:8).
   H. We have great resources—modern technology.

II. **The Church's Need.**
   A. We need New Testament Christianity.
      1. With born-again members (John 3:3).
      2. With faithful stewards (1 Peter 4:10).
      3. With diligent servants (2 Tim. 2:24).
   B. We need a willingness to put God first.
      1. To be what God wants.
      2. To do what God wants.
      3. To go where God wants.
   C. We need open-minded members.
      1. Open to the call of God to go.
      2. Open to the call of God to give.

2

Reaching Out

Matthew 28:18–20

I. Our Command Is Unmistakable.

A. Notice the four verbs in the command.

1. *Go*—movement of the body.
   a. From one place to another—missions.
   b. From one person to another—witness.
2. *Teach* (make)—movement of the heart.
3. *Baptize*—movement of the water.
4. *Teach*—movement of the mind.

B. Notice the plan that Jesus had in mind.

1. It is a mathematical plan:
   a. One win one, two win two, three win three, etc.
   b. In twelve months this would equal thirty-two.
   c. In twenty-four months this would equal 512.
2. It is a complete plan—discipling.

II. Unconcern Is Inexcusable.

A. Unconcern implies three things.

1. An absence of God's love in the heart.
2. A disrespect for the Word of God.
3. A disregard for one's fellow man.

B. Parable of the Good Samaritan (Luke 10:30–37).

III. All Resources Should Be Available.

A. A church should stretch to the limits of its capability.

B. A church's main business is reaching people for Jesus.

C. A church's business is the Christian's business.

D. A church's plan should be the same as Jesus' plan.

1. We are to win the lost to Jesus.
2. We are to train the saved to serve.

3
Be at Peace

Mark 4:35–41

The problems of life can be compared to a storm. Notice why the disciples should have been at peace.

I. Because of the Position They Were In.
- A. They were in the perfect will of God.
  1. Jesus told them to cross the lake (v. 35).
  2. They were acting on a divine word.
     - a. They had acted on his word before (Luke 5:4).
     - b. Gideon had acted on God's Word (Judges 7:7, 9).
     - c. Man at Bethesda acted on his word (John 5:8–9).
     - d. We acted on a word when we were saved.
  3. Jesus was already in the boat.
- B. We Christians should not be fearful (2 Tim. 1:7).
  1. If we are in the right position (1 John 1:7).
  2. We must not be preoccupied with the world (Matt. 6:19).

II. Because of the Person They Were With.
- A. The disciples made one mistake.
  1. They overestimated the size of the problem.
     - a. They thought they were perishing.
     - b. In a storm, the roll indicator on a ship is the center of attention.
     - c. Notice Elisha's servant (2 Kings 6:15–17).
     - d. Sentence was already passed on Peter (Acts 12:1–11).
  2. Exaggerating our problems is a common human trait.
     - a. It is self-centered.
     - b. It reduces our energy for more worthwhile concerns.
- B. The disciples did one thing right.
  1. They went to the right person.
  2. We should always go to Jesus with our needs.
     - a. He promised to be with us (Matt. 28:20).
     - b. He promised never to leave us (Heb. 13:5).
  3. Having Jesus present makes a difference (Acts 27:22–25).

4

Does Jesus Care?

Mark 4:36–41

The disciples asked Jesus, "Teacher, do you not care if we perish?" There are times when we wonder if anyone cares. The Bible reveals the human predicament. Life's experiences confirm this predicament. Society seems only to add to it and people seem uncaring about it. The church has even been called into question. This only leaves Jesus. Does he care?

I. **See What Jesus Did by Coming (Phil. 2:7–8).**
   A. He gave up the glory he had from the beginning.
   B. He assumed the limitations of humanity.
      1. He can understand our infirmities (Heb. 4:15).
      2. He was tempted like we are (Heb. 4:15).
   C. He became a servant of men.

II. **See What Jesus Did While He Was Here.**
   A. Our predicament (harassed, helpless, like sheep without a shepherd) is seen in Matthew 9:36.
   B. Jesus was moved with compassion.
      1. He healed the sick (Matt. 14:14).
      2. He became their shepherd (Mark 6:34).
      3. He wept at Lazarus's tomb (John 11:35).
      4. He delayed his trip to the cross to deal with individual needs (Luke 18–19).

III. **See What Jesus Did on Calvary.**
   A. Jesus gave his life for sinners.
      1. His life was not taken (John 10:18).
      2. He opened not his mouth (Acts 8:32).
      3. His words at Gethsemane (Matt. 26:53).
   B. Jesus really does care for us.

5 Discipleship

Luke 14:25–33

I. **What Is a Disciple?**
   A. It does not mean simply "one who is saved."
   B. It means "one who has been disciplined."
      1. Discipline means "bring under control."
      2. A disciple is one brought under the control of Jesus.

II. **How Do We Become Disciples?**
   A. First, we must receive Jesus as Savior.
   B. Then we must decide to be a disciple.
      1. We are challenged by the Word (vv. 25–26).
      2. We are convicted by the Holy Spirit.
      3. We must voluntarily subject ourselves to Christ.
         a. Wives are to be in subjection to their husbands.
         b. Parents are to bring children into subjection.
         c. Christians must subject themselves to Jesus.
   C. It is deciding to make Jesus Lord of our lives.

III. **What Does It Cost to Be a Disciple?**
   A. Jesus points this out in the text.
      1. There is cost involved in discipleship.
      2. We won't be able to do everything we would like.
      3. We won't be able to do some things others do.
      4. We may be called on to make great sacrifices.
   B. Jesus said we should count the cost.
      1. He used two examples to illustrate.
         a. The man building a tower (Luke 14:28–30).
         b. The king going to war (Luke 14:31–33).
      2. Two things happen when one is unable to pay the price.
         a. He is ridiculed—as in the case of the tower.
         b. He capitulates—as in the case of the king.

6

How Important Are You?

Luke 15:3–7

Everyone likes to feel important and wanted. How important are you to God?

I. The Parable of the Lost Sheep.

- A. Notice how important that one sheep was.
  1. The shepherd considered it a loss.
     - a. Losing things of no value is not considered a loss and has little effect on us. A penny in a parking lot is often ignored.
     - b. Losing a valuable item such as health, loved ones, business, etc., greatly affects us.
  2. The shepherd was concerned over the loss. He left the flock to seek the lost sheep. He didn't stop until he had found the lost sheep.
- B. Three reasons the shepherd rejoiced.
  1. Something important had been recovered.
  2. His efforts had been rewarded.
  3. He had fulfilled his responsibility.

II. The Application of the Parable.

- A. How important are you to God?
  1. Individuals have always mattered to God.
     - a. Jesus often dealt with one person in a crowd (Zacchaeus, Bartimaeus, woman with the issue of blood, etc.).
     - b. Special efforts were made to reach one person (Cornelius, Paul, Ethiopian eunuch, etc.).
  2. How can you know that God cares about you?
     - a. Because of what he did (John 3:16).
     - b. Because of what he promises (John 6:37).
- B. How should you react to such concern?
  1. You should invite him in (Rev. 3:20).
  2. You should love him (1 John 4:19).

7

A Man Named Nicodemus

John 3:1–21

I. **Nicodemus Was a Religious Man (v. 1b).**
   A. That would seem to be to his credit.
      1. Many people think religion is the goal of our spiritual search.
      2. Others study religions and select one to follow.
   B. Religion has never been the goal.
      1. Almost everyone has a religion (Buddhism, humanism, Hinduism, etc.).
      2. The goal is to become a new person in Christ.

II. **Nicodemus Was a Curious Man (v. 2).**
   A. He was curious about the man Jesus.
      1. Whether he was the Messiah.
      2. Whether he was a messenger.
   B. He was curious about the teachings of Jesus.

III. **Nicodemus Was a Confused Man (vv. 3–4).**
   A. He was confused about what Jesus said.
      1. Jesus said one must be born again.
      2. Jesus knocked the props out from under Nicodemus.
         a. Because he thought being a son of Abraham was enough.
         b. And he thought being religious was sufficient.
   B. He was confused about spiritual truths.
      1. He tried to understand spiritual truths intellectually.
      2. Spiritual truths can be real but not understood.

IV. **Nicodemus Was a Fortunate Man (vv. 5–9).**
   A. He received further instruction.
      1. Jesus made sure Nicodemus understood the truth about spiritual rebirth.
      2. Some are not so fortunate (Matt. 13:13–15).
   B. He received a word of comfort (v. 7).

V. **Nicodemus Was a Sinner in Need (vv. 10–21).**
   A. He was reprimanded by Jesus.

    1. Because he should have known these things (v. 10).
    2. Because he doubted the words of Jesus (v. 11).
    3. Because his spiritual growth was hindered (v. 12).
B. He was preached to by Jesus.
    1. About the incarnation (v. 13).
    2. About the atonement (v. 14).
    3. About faith in the Savior (vv. 15–20).

8

Believe in Jesus

John 11:1–27

We use the words *faith* and *belief* interchangeably. We use them in referring to two distinct areas: when we are talking about salvation, and when we are talking about Christian living.

I. Jesus Was Invited into a Problem.

- A. The sisters made sure he was aware (v. 3).
- B. This is always the right course of action (Matt. 11:28; Ps. 50:15; 91:15).

II. Jesus Was Inclined to Solve the Problem.

- A. He declared his intention (v. 11).
- B. He is inclined to meet your need (Matt. 6:25–33).
- C. He acted in his own time and way (vv. 6, 15).
    1. Things don't always happen the way we want.
        - a. The sisters wanted Lazarus to get well (v. 21).
        - b. Rich young ruler never expected the demand (Luke 18:23).
        - c. Naaman objected to dipping in Jordan (2 Kings 5:10–11).
        - d. John the Baptist was not what people expected (Luke 7:24).
    2. God's ways are not our ways (Isa. 55:8–9).
    3. God has his own time schedule (Acts 17:26).

III. We Are Not Always Inclined to Believe.

- A. Pessimism is the beginning of the end of faith.
    1. Faith ceases when complaining begins.
    2. Faith, by nature, is optimistic.
- B. What seems like faith is sometimes unbelief.
    1. The sisters implied situation now hopeless (v. 37).
    2. Notice the same situation in verses 20–27.
    3. Martha expressed doctrinal belief.
        - a. Doctrinal belief and trusting God are not the same.
        - b. One can be orthodox in belief but weak in faith.
        - c. Doctrine doesn't help much in times of need.
        - d. Jesus, the person, is our help in time of need.

9

Delivering

Acts 2:22–24

Delivering is big business today (UPS, Federal Express, etc.). In a sense, God is in the delivery business.

I. The Father Delivered the Son into the Presence of Man.

- A. The gospel is a spiritual gift certificate.
  1. A gift certificate is a promissory note. The gift has already been paid for and is yours for the claiming.
  2. The gospel promises salvation for the claiming.
- B. Jesus was sent to live among men.
  1. Jesus was sent to die for the sins of men.
  2. Jesus was sent by the Father (John 3:16).

II. The Son Delivers Sinners into the Presence of the Father.

- A. Notice the custom of ancient courts.
  1. A steward controlled audiences with the king.
     - a. None could see the king without the steward's permission.
     - b. Esther's risk was in bypassing the steward.
  2. Joseph was the steward of Pharaoh.
- B. There is a mediator between God and man.
  1. None can come into God's presence but by him.
  2. In the Old Testament the high priest was the mediator.
     - a. He alone could enter the Holy of Holies.
     - b. He dealt with God on behalf of the people.
  3. Jesus Christ is the sinner's high priest.
     - a. "No man cometh unto the Father . . ." (John 14:6).
     - b. Jesus deals with God on our behalf.

III. The Church Delivers Sinners into the Presence of Jesus.

- A. That is the mission of the church.
  1. To introduce sinners to the Savior.
  2. This is done through the preaching of the gospel (Rom. 10:14–15; Matt. 28:18–20).
- B. It is hard for sinners to be saved.

1. The righteous are scarcely saved (1 Peter 4:18).
2. They need all the help they can get.
    a. That is why the church is in the world.
    b. The church is in the delivery business (Luke 14:23).

10

Time on Our Hands

Acts 9:31

I. **The Church Had a Time of Peace.**
   A. God had given them a rest.
      1. The church had suffered severe persecution.
         a. Many believers had been imprisoned (Acts 5:18).
         b. Stephen had been stoned to death (Acts 7:59).
         c. Saul had waged a one-man war (Acts 9:1).
      2. God had given them a respite.
         a. He dealt with external problems by converting Saul (Paul).
         b. He dealt with internal problems by removing Ananias and Sapphira (Acts 5:5, 10).
   B. Churches need periods of rest sometimes.
      1. A rest from some things to give attention to other things.
      2. This does not mean a rest from labors.

II. **The Church Had a Time of Strengthening.**
   A. This was one of the reasons for the rest.
   B. The areas where strengthening was needed.
      1. They needed physical strengthening.
      2. They needed their faith strengthened (Rom. 15:1).
      3. They needed doctrinal strengthening.
      4. They needed organizational strengthening (Titus 1:5).
      5. They needed their fellowship strengthened.

III. **The Church Had a Time of Growth.**
   A. To what can we attribute their growth?
      1. It can be attributed to their attitude.
      2. It can be attributed to their program.
         a. A program of prayer (Acts 1:24; 6:6; 12:5).
         b. A program of Bible study (Acts 2:42).
         c. A program of fellowship (Acts 2:42).
         d. A program of evangelism (Acts 4:31; 12:24).
   B. The church should always be advancing.

11
Ready and Willing

Romans 1:13–16

Christians are faced with a great challenge. Paul said he was ready to meet the challenge.

I. Several Things About Paul's Readiness.
- A. He was ready from the day of conversion (Acts 9:6).
- B. He was ready with everything he had (v. 15).
- C. He was ready for any service, any place (v. 15).
- D. He was ready to the end of his life (Phil. 3:13–16).

II. Why Paul Was So Ready and Willing.
- A. Not because he was ignorant of the cost (2 Tim. 4:6).
- B. Not because he was better trained or more gifted.
- C. He was a genuinely converted man (2 Cor. 5:17).
- D. He was a sanctified man (2 Tim. 2:21).
- E. He was a man of strong convictions.
  1. He believed all are sinners and lost (Rom. 3:23; 6:23).
  2. He believed the gospel was the remedy (v. 16).
  3. He believed he was a steward of that gospel (1 Cor. 4:1–2).
- F. He was a man of compassion.

III. The Result of Paul's Readiness.
- A. He was a very busy man.
- B. He was an effective, successful servant.
  1. He knew his work was ordained of God.
  2. He knew heaven's resources were behind it.
  3. A salesman must be sold on his product.

IV. God Needs People Now Who Will Accept the Challenge.
- A. The challenge of Christian leadership.
- B. The challenge of faithful stewardship.

12
Areas of Judgment

Romans 14:11–12

Life is an individual responsibility. This is cause for giving attention to some areas.

I. **Attention to Our Time (Matt. 20:6–7).**
   A. There is reproach in the language (v. 6).
      1. The eleventh hour is close to the end of opportunity.
      2. Their excuse—"No man has hired us."
   B. The implication is that it is never too late.

II. **Attention to Our Action (1 Sam. 2:3).**
   A. All actions are not immediately judged.
      1. All human actions will be judged.
      2. God himself is the judge of our actions.
   B. Justice strikes fear in some, joy in others.

III. **Attention to Our Ways (Pss. 1:6; 119:168).**
   A. People are known by their way of life.
   B. The Lord knows the way every person has chosen (Ps. 1:1–2).
      1. This implies that we have a choice in life.
      2. This will be confirmed in judgment (Ps. 1:5).

IV. **Attention to Our Words (Matt. 12:36).**
   A. The Bible has much to say about our words.
      1. Peter said to refrain your tongue from evil (1 Peter 3:10).
      2. James said the tongue "is an unruly evil" (James 3:8).
   B. Words reveal the state of one's heart (Matt. 12:34).

V. **Attention to Our Works (1 Cor. 3:13).**
   A. We should be diligent about the quantity of work.
   B. We should be diligent about the quality of work.

VI. **Attention to Our Money (Mark 12:41).**
   A. Jesus' action indicated that he was interested.
   B. God takes note of how we use our wealth.

VII. **Attention to Our Life (Rom. 14:7–8).**
   A. Life is a trust, not a possession.
   B. Life as a trust involves accountability.

13
It's the Greatest

1 Corinthians 13

The "greatest" means there is nothing better. What is the greatest thing in the world?

- **I. The World Holds Many Things Up Before Us.**
  - A. The world says, "Seek fame and popularity."
    1. This quest begins in grammar school and before.
    2. Many people become paranoid when their popularity is threatened.
  - B. The world says, "Seek prosperity."
    1. Success is measured in dollars and cents.
    2. Those who don't get it are failures.
  - C. The world says, "Get to the top of the heap."
- **II. Religion Holds Many Things Up Before Us.**
  - A. Religion says, "Observe all the rules and exercises."
  - B. Religion says, "Be benevolent" (v. 3).
  - C. Religion says, "Manifest spiritual gifts" (vv. 1–2a).
    1. Seek the gifts of tongues, prophecies, etc.
    2. When you have these, you have arrived.
  - D. Religion says, "Have faith" (v. 2b).
    1. Believe and everything will be yours.
    2. Believe it and it will happen.
- **III. What Is the Greatest Thing in the World?**
  - A. Paul said love is the greatest (v. 13).
    1. It is the basic, motivating attribute of God (1 John 4:16; John 3:16).
    2. It is the first among God's commandments (Matt. 22:36–40).
    3. It is the fulfilling of the law (Gal. 5:14).
    4. It is the proof of salvation (1 John 3:14).
  - B. Love opened the door of heaven for us (John 3:16).

14

What Will We Do in Heaven?

1 Corinthians 13:9–10, 12

I. **Contemplate the Works and Glory of God.**
   A. We will see the universe as we have never seen it.
      1. The psalmist marveled at God's works (Ps. 8:3–9).
         a. He had not even seen what we have seen.
         b. We have seen only a small part of God's works.
      2. We will see parts of the universe hitherto unseen.
      3. We will see events of history hitherto unknown (Rev. 15:2–3).
   B. We will know God as we have never known him.
      1. One can know God today in salvation.
      2. We will someday see God in all of his glory.
         a. The glory of his holiness and righteousness.
         b. The glory of his love and mercy.

II. **Grow in Our Faculties and Character.**
   A. In this life our growth is hindered.
      1. We are preoccupied with the things of the world.
      2. We are hindered by the weakness of the flesh.
   B. In heaven our growth will not be hindered.
      1. Our flesh will be changed (1 Cor. 15:51–52).
      2. Our desires will be altered.
      3. Our holiness will be complete.
      4. Our graces and virtues will be perfected.
      5. Our understanding and love will be expanded.

III. **Be Employed in Worship and Service.**
   A. Adam was given a work in the beginning.
      1. He was given some responsibility.
      2. This reveals God's intention for man.
   B. Heaven will not be a place for idleness.
      1. We will be given work to do.
      2. We will be engaged in worship (Rev. 7:15).

15
You Can Be Different

2 Corinthians 5:17

Your life can change, be different. Paul had experienced dramatic changes. This was a result of an encounter with Jesus Christ. Notice the changes that Christ can make.

I. He Can Change Your Status.
- A. Everyone stands someplace in relation to God.
- B. Notice what happens when you meet Jesus Christ.
  1. Pass from death to life (1 John 3:14).
  2. Pass from darkness to light (1 Peter 2:9).
  3. Pass from condemnation to justification (John 3:18).

II. He Can Change Your Destination.
- A. Sign on roadside: "Where will you spend eternity?"
  1. The Bible answers this clearly for all men.
  2. Satan tries to confuse you about this.
     - a. Purgatory, reincarnation, oblivion, etc.
     - b. He tries to keep you from salvation (2 Cor. 4:3–4).
- B. Jesus changes your eternal destination (John 14:2–3).

III. He Can Change Your Purpose.
- A. What is your reason for living?
  1. Many live just to have a good time.
  2. Some don't have any purpose.
- B. Jesus gives you a real reason for living.
  1. It is to please and glorify God.
  2. You are an ambassador for the King of kings (2 Cor. 5:20).

IV. He Can Change Your Outlook.
- A. Suicide is the number-two killer of teenagers.
  1. Why would young people do this?
  2. They see life as pressure, distress, and defeat.
- B. Jesus gives us a better quality of life (John 10:10).

16

Blessing

2 Corinthians 9:6–15

This text is a great lesson on giving. This text is also a great lesson on thanksgiving.

I. Notice the Principle of Blessing (v. 6).
- A. You receive in proportion to what you give.
  1. Some call this the "seed faith" principle.
  2. Paul used a farmer as an illustration.
     - a. If he plants few seeds, he reaps a small crop.
     - b. If he plants many seeds, he reaps a large crop.
- B. God blesses according to our generosity.

II. Notice the Premise of Blessing (vv. 7–8a).
- A. God loves a cheerful giver (v. 7).
  1. This has to do with attitudes.
  2. We are not to give out of constraint or duty.
- B. God is able to make grace abound (v. 8).
  1. TEV says "give you more than you need."
  2. This will allow you to give more (see v. 7).

III. Notice the Purpose of Blessing (vv. 8b, 12a).
- A. So we will have to give to good causes (v. 8b).
  1. The blessings may come through natural channels.
  2. The blessings come for God's purposes.
- B. So the needs of God's people can be met (v. 12a).

IV. Notice the Promise of Blessing (vv. 8, 10b).
- A. God will provide what you need (v. 8).
  1. What you need for yourself and your family.
  2. What you need to give (v. 11a).
- B. God will bless what you give (v. 10b).

V. Notice the Product of Blessing (vv. 12–14).
- A. It produces an outpouring of gratitude (v. 12b).

        1. The givers will give glory to God (v. 13).
        2. The recipients will give glory to God (v. 13).
    B. It causes people to have affection for you (v. 14).
    C. It moves people to pray for you (v. 14).

VI. Notice the Pinnacle of Blessing (v. 15).
    A. One blessing stands out above all others.
        1. Paul calls it the "unspeakable gift."
        2. Paul refers to eternal life in Christ.
    B. God wants to bless you today.

17

Areas of Deception

Galatians 3:1

Paul suggested that the Galatians were "bewitched," or easily attracted to false teachings. Many people are also being so deceived today.

I. In the Area of Salvation.

A. What does Satan tell us about salvation?

1. There is more than one way to be saved.
2. All that is required is to do your best.
3. You will be saved if you are faithful to your religious practices.
4. If you believe in God, you will be saved.
5. If you come from a Christian family, you are in.

B. What does God say about salvation?

1. Everyone is a sinner and needs to be saved (John 3:3).
2. Jesus died on the cross to save us (1 Cor. 15:3).
3. We are saved by faith in Jesus alone (John 3:16).

II. In the Area of Service.

A. What does Satan tell us about service?

1. Someone else will do the job.
2. You don't have the time to serve.
3. You don't have the talents to serve.

B. What does God tell us about service?

1. Every Christian is expected to serve.
   a. The branch that doesn't bear fruit will be cut off (John 15:1–2).
   b. We are ambassadors for Christ (2 Cor. 5:20).
2. Every Christian is a part of a mission (Luke 24:45–48).

III. In the Area of Sin.

A. What does Satan tell us about sin?

1. There is no such thing as sin.
   a. You are being deprived of pleasure if you don't do as you please.
   b. Do whatever makes you happy.

2. There is really nothing bad about sin.
    a. It is bad only to the "old fashioned."
    b. God is more concerned with social issues.

B. What does God tell us about sin?
    1. Sin is a reality to be dealt with.
        a. Model prayer: "forgive us our sins. . . ."
        b. "Go and sin no more" (John 8:11).
    2. Sin is serious in God's eyes.
    3. There is forgiveness through Jesus Christ.

18

What Being a Child of God Means

Galatians 4:4–7

Believers become the sons of God (John 1:12). We are adopted into God's family (v. 5). What does it mean to be a child of God?

I. All of Our Past Debts Are Covered.
- A. Our new family accepts responsibility for us.
- B. As sinners we have a staggering debt.
  1. The debt is beyond our ability to pay.
  2. God assumes accountability for our debt.
     - a. "Sent forth his Son . . . to redeem us . . ." (vv. 4–5).
     - b. We come into God's family debt free.

II. All of Our Future Blessings Are Assured.
- A. Two things happen to an adopted child.
  1. The child becomes a charge of a new family.
  2. The child becomes an heir of a new family.
- B. The same things happen to Christians.
  1. We become God's charges.
     - a. Our well-being becomes his responsibility.
     - b. Our nurture and growth become his concern.
  2. We become God's heirs (Rom. 8:16–17a).
     - a. Every blessing that God has becomes ours.
     - b. Our inheritance is assured (1 Peter 1:3–5).

III. All of Our Responsibilities Are Changed.
- A. We are expected to live up to family standards.
  1. Certain things are expected of family members.
     - a. These involve chores, conduct, manners, etc.
     - b. Alexander the Great said to a sloppy soldier named Alexander, "Change your ways or change your name!"
  2. Certain things are expected of God's children.

B. We assume the obligations of the new family.
    1. The obligation to attend family gatherings.
    2. The obligation to share the gospel.
    3. The obligation to study and grow strong.

19

Edification

Ephesians 4:11–16

Edification means "building up or growing up." There are two areas in which a church can grow: in quantity—growing in number; in quality—growing in stature. The goal is to produce perfect people (v. 13).

I. The Basis for Edification—Speaking the Truth.
- A. Truth is the foundation for all growth (John 17:17).
- B. The Bible therefore is of utmost importance.

II. The Motivation for Edification—In Love.
- A. Love is the reason we seek to grow.
- B. The church at Corinth was not growing.
  1. It was gifted for growth (1 Cor. 12).
  2. It was without love (1 Cor. 13).

III. The Direction of Edification—Grow Up into Him.
- A. The fullness of Christ is our goal (v. 13).
- B. Not everything contributes to this.
  1. Not all lawful things (1 Cor. 6:1).
  2. Not all religious activity.

IV. The Scope of Edification—In All Things.
- A. We are to grow in all areas.
- B. We are to grow at all times (Phil. 3:12).

V. A Prerequisite to Edification—Whole Body Fitly Joined.
- A. Unity of believers is necessary to growth (Gal. 6:2).
- B. Unity of believers depends on unity with Christ.

VI. A Necessity for Edification—Every Joint Supplieth.
- A. Growth is dependent on mutual ministry.
  1. Every believer has a contribution to make.
  2. Every believer has a contribution to receive.
- B. Growth is dependent on every believer's involvement.

VII. The Goal of Edification—Increase of the Body.
- A. We are to grow spiritually to numerically.
- B. Quality is to contribute toward quantity.

20
Expressing Gratitude

Ephesians 5:20

When people are grateful, they will show it by attitudes and actions.

I. **Attitudes and Action Toward Other People.**
   A. Jesus spoke of the judgment (Matt. 25:34–46).
      1. It will not be based on how religious we are.
      2. It will be based on how we treat other people.
   B. Jesus spoke of two creditors (Matt. 18:23–35).
      1. The master expected the servant to forgive also.
         a. Freely ye have received, freely give (Matt. 10:8).
         b. Much will be required (Luke 12:48).
      2. This calls us to compassion and forgiveness.

II. **Attitudes and Action Toward the Church.**
   A. To love Jesus is to love the church.
      1. The church is the body of Christ (Eph. 1:22–23).
      2. Jesus loved the church (Eph. 5:25).
   B. Who would believe a father loved his family if he came home only on Easter and Christmas?
   C. Our attitude toward the church should be the same as our attitude toward Jesus.
      1. We should be willing to serve it.
      2. We should be willing to give to it.
      3. We should be willing to listen to it.

III. **Attitudes and Actions Toward Life.**
   A. Paul spoke of man's problem (Rom. 1:20–21).
      1. It is not the mystery of God's existence.
      2. It is man's ingratitude to God.
   B. The signs of man's ingratitude.
      1. His rejection of Jesus as Savior.
      2. His refusal to be reconciled to God.

21

The Need to Grow

Philippians 1:9–11

I. Three Areas in Which We Need to Grow.
- A. We need to grow in love (v. 9).
  1. All else is meaningless (1 Cor. 13:1–3).
  2. Qualities of love (1 Cor. 13:4–7).
  3. Everything else fades away (1 Cor. 13:8–13).
- B. We need to grow in true knowledge (v. 9).
  1. This is the ability to rightly decide.
  2. Every church needs to be able to rightly discern.
  3. Every Christian needs to be able to rightly discern.

II. Four Reasons We Need This Growth.
- A. To be able to choose what is best (v. 10).
- B. To be free of blame in the judgment (v. 10b).
  1. We will be judged on our growth (1 Cor. 3:13).
  2. God expects growth in everyone (John 15:1–12).
- C. To be filled with good qualities (v. 11a).
  1. Man cannot produce what God considers good.
  2. The Holy Spirit must produce these qualities.
- D. To glorify and praise God (v. 11b).
  1. God's word to Satan about Job (Job 1:8).
  2. God's desire for us (Matt. 5:16).

III. The Way to Grow in These Areas.
- A. Through commitment to Jesus Christ.
- B. Through a commitment to honesty (Eph. 4:15).
- C. Through a commitment to God's Word.
  1. One must desire it to grow (1 Peter 2:1–2).
  2. A commitment to live by the Word.

22

The Christian Aim

Philippians 3:13–14

There are three things every Christian should do.

I. Forget Things that Are Behind.

- A. Forget past difficulties.
  1. Sacrifices made in the past.
  2. Obstacles faced in the past.
- B. Forget past failures and sins.
  1. Jesus' words to Simon Peter (Luke 22:32).
  2. Runners in a race should never look back.
- C. Forget past attractions.
  1. Attractions of worldly success.
  2. Attractions of worldly pleasures.

II. Reach for Things that Are Before.

- A. Reach for victory.
  1. The crown or prize goes to the victor (1 Cor. 9:24).
  2. Victory over sin and death.
- B. Reach for success.
  1. Christian success is to glorify God (1 Cor. 10:31).
  2. Christian success is to run with patience (Heb. 12:1).
- C. Reach for holiness.
  1. There must be a beginning—yield (Rom. 6:19).
  2. There must be a continuation—perfecting (2 Cor. 7:1).

III. Press Toward the Mark.

- A. Press toward the finish line.
  1. This is the goal of all sports.
  2. Keep your eye on the ribbon—single-eyed (Matt. 6:22).
- B. Press toward faithfulness.
  1. Requirements of a steward (1 Cor. 4:2).
  2. Faithfulness to the high calling of God.
- C. Press toward heaven.
  1. Our call is *from* heaven *to* heaven.
     - a. John was told "come up hither . . ." (Rev. 4:1).
     - b. Church's call seen in 1 Thessalonians 4:16.
  2. Our crown is in heaven (1 Peter 1:4; 2 Tim. 4:8).

23
How to Stand

Colossians 2:6–7

I. **Learn to Live in Union with Christ.**
  A. First, we must become one with Christ.
    1. Text says, "As ye have therefore received Christ" (v. 6).
    2. We become one with Christ when we are saved.
  B. It is similar to living in the state of marriage.
    1. Two individuals commit to each other (see 1 Cor. 6:16b–17).
    2. They are no longer free to go their separate ways.

II. **Keep Your Roots Deep in Christ.**
  A. A tree depends on its roots.
    1. The roots draw life from the soil.
    2. The roots give stability to the tree.
  B. We must be rooted deeply and firmly in Christ.
    1. Text means "keep" our roots in him (v. 7).
    2. We draw our life from him (John 15:4).

III. **Build Your Life on Christ.**
  A. Houses need a solid foundation.
    1. A house cannot stand without one.
    2. Parable of two builders (Matt. 7:24–27).
  B. Lives need a solid foundation, too.
    1. There is a foundation laid (1 Cor. 3:11).
    2. Hymn: "On Christ, the Solid Rock, I Stand."

IV. **Become Stronger in Faith.**
  A. Faith means having confidence in God.
    1. It is easy to trust when things go well.
    2. In life, things don't always go well (John 16:33).
  B. Faith needs to be strengthened (Rom. 10:17).

V. **Be Filled with Thanksgiving.**
  A. This does not refer to outward expression.
  B. This refers to an inward condition of the heart.
    1. This will naturally produce the outward expression.
    2. The inward must precede the outward (Matt. 15:18).

24

Who Are You?

Colossians 3:12–17 (TEV)

In some situations people wear name-tags. This is a means of identification and a way of introduction. All of us have a name by which we are known.

I. Christians Have a Unique Title (v. 12).

- A. How did we come to be the "people of God?"
  1. Not by natural birth (John 1:3).
  2. Not by joining a church or other group.
  3. Not by mentally accepting the Bible.
  4. God loved us and chose us (v. 12).
- B. We were adopted by God (Gal. 4:3–5).

II. Christians Have Some Personal Obligations (vv. 12b–17).

- A. "So then" refers to previous phrase (v. 12b).
  1. The phrase "you are the people of God."
  2. The phrase "He loved you and chose you."
- B. "You must" appears four times in the text.
  1. It is in the imperative sense—an absolute.
  2. It is the same phrase Jesus used in John 3:7.
  3. It leaves no options or alternatives.
- C. Notice the obligations placed on us.
  1. Conduct in living (vv. 12–14).
  2. Conduct in worship (vv. 15–17).

III. Christians Have a Gauge by Which to Check Themselves (v. 15a).

- A. The peace of God is our gauge.
  1. There are two kinds of peace.
     - a. Peace in the individual heart.
     - b. Peace within the body—the church.
  2. God intends for peace to rule in both places.
- B. The peace of God is disturbed by wrong conduct.

25

Faith, Love, and Hope

1 Thessalonians 1:2–3

Paul remembered three things about them (v. 3). Recall the church at Ephesus (Rev. 2:1–2). The Lord knew of their works, labor, and patience. No mention is made of their work being of faith, love, or hope. It is possible for a work not to be the result of these qualities.

I. What Is a Work of Faith?
- A. It is a work initiated by God.
  1. Some work is clearly God's will (missions).
  2. Some work requires seeking direction.
- B. It is a work carried out by God.
  1. It has the power of God behind it (2 Thess. 1:11).
  2. We exercise faith, God exerts power.
- C. The results of the work are of God.
  1. God gives the increase (1 Cor. 3:6).
  2. Paul and Apollos were involved.

II. What Is a Labor of Love?
- A. It is a labor which is born out of love.
  1. It comes into being because somebody cares.
  2. This is the labor from which churches are born.
- B. It is labor which is carried on in love.
  1. It is carried on because someone loves God.
  2. It is carried on because someone loves people.
- C. It is a labor given value by love.
  1. Labor can be of little value (1 Cor. 13:2–3; 3:8–11).
  2. The words of Jesus are sobering (Matt. 7:22–23).

III. What Is a Patience of Hope?
- A. Note the meaning of the two words.
  1. Patience means "calmly enduring."
  2. Hope means "prospect of something unseen."
  3. As we labor, we "calmly endure while waiting for something yet unseen."
- B. The patience of hope keeps us going.
  1. Through the tests and trials of life.
  2. Through the difficulties of work.

26

Getting It All Together

1 Thessalonians 5:23

Definitions of modern life. Some say "sophisticated," "hip," or "way out." Religiously, life is "fragmented"—"without a unifying force." Some would say it is "strung out." We need to get our lives together. Our Lord's ministry was aimed at this. The word *saved* can also be translated "whole."

I. Jesus Is Interested in the Whole Person.

- A. We tend to divide life into parts.
  1. We separate the physical, mental, and spiritual.
  2. We separate the religious from the secular.
  3. It is church on Sunday but business as usual on Monday.
- B. Churches even tend to do this.
  1. Some concentrate on evangelism and neglect ministry.
  2. Some concentrate on ministry and neglect evangelism.
  3. Jesus is interested in the whole person.

II. Jesus Is Interested in the Whole Life.

- A. Christians are often accused of hypocrisy.
  1. Everyone acts below standard sometimes.
  2. No life should be judged by isolated incidents.
  3. "He that is without sin among you, let him first cast . . ." (John 8:7).
- B. Jesus is interested in our total lives.
  1. He did not reject Peter because of mistakes.
  2. Read Paul's statements about judgment (1 Cor. 3).
  3. Every great Bible character had faults.

III. Jesus Is Interested in the Whole Church.

- A. He wants wholeness in the body (church).
  1. Ephesians 1:10 speaks of gathering "together in one."
  2. Song: "We Are One in the Spirit."
- B. He wants unity of spirit above all else.
  1. Above unity of doctrine, program, or methods.
  2. He is interested in your personal relationships.

27

The Thessalonians

2 Thessalonians 2:13–17

I. **Paul's Statement About Them (vv. 13–14).**
   A. He said they were loved of God (v. 13).
      1. Three assurances Paul had of God's love.
         a. What Jesus did on the cross (no greater love).
         b. What God himself had told Paul (revelation).
         c. What God had told others (Scripture).
      2. We can tell others that God loves them.
   B. He said they were chosen of God (v. 13).
      1. Chosen—the doctrine of election.
      2. Chosen—the doctrine of foreknowledge.
      3. Chosen through belief of the truth (v. 13b).
   C. He said they were called of God (v. 14).
      1. God calls sinners through gospel preaching.
      2. Everyone who hears has been called of God.
         a. He has had an invitation to be saved.
         b. He has had an opportunity to be saved.
         c. Some who did not respond to the gospel were Agrippa, rich young ruler, Felix, Festus.
         d. Some who did respond to the gospel were Cornelius, Philippian jailor, Ethiopian eunuch, Paul.

II. **Paul's Prayer for Them.**
   A. That God would help them live a good life (v. 15).
      1. Paul knew this life was God's will.
      2. Paul knew this life was difficult.
      3. This life consists of words and action.
   B. Two things in particular Paul prayed for (vv. 16–17).
      1. That God would encourage them.
      2. That God would strengthen them.

28
A Time to Refocus

2 Thessalonians 3:5

"Direct" means to refocus that which is blurred or not clear. Christians sometimes stray from God in heart, grow weary of well doing, and grow slack in their duties. Paul prayed for the Thessalonians to get refocused.

I. Refocus Their Love for God.
- A. Christians should love God above all else.
  1. Deuteronomy 6:5 commands such love.
  2. Jesus called it the first and greatest commandment (Matt. 22:38).
- B. Christians sometimes fall out of love with God.
  1. The world steals our affection (Matt. 6:24; Luke 8:14).
  2. The devil undermines our love (1 Peter 5:8).
  3. We fail to nourish that love.
- C. Christians need to be directed back to loving God.

II. Refocus Their Waiting.
- A. There are three kinds of patience in Scripture.
  1. Laboring patience (Rom. 2:7; Luke 8:15).
  2. Suffering patience (Gal. 6:9; Job 2:10).
  3. Waiting patience (Heb. 6:12; Rom. 8:25).
- B. Waiting patience is a duty of the saints.
  1. We must surrender to God's timetable.
  2. We are insubordinate when we are impatient (Exod. 32:1).
  3. We must wait on the Lord (Ps. 37:7).
- C. Christians sometimes do not wait patiently.
  1. We take matters into our own hands (1 Sam. 13:8–13).
  2. We forsake our duties and/or work.
- D. Christians need to be directed back to patience.
  1. We must patiently wait for the coming of the Lord.
  2. Paul prayed that the Thessalonians might be helped to do that.

29

Instructions for Prayer

1 Timothy 2:1–8

I. We Ought to Pray.

A. Paul urged Timothy to pray.
   1. He listed prayer as a matter of urgency (v. 1a).
   2. He expressed it as a matter of duty (v. 8a).

B. Prayer is a basic Christian duty.
   1. Scripture tells us to pray (Eph. 6:18).
   2. It is God's will for us to pray (Matt. 5:44; 6:9).

II. We Ought to Pray for Each Other.

A. Pray for all people in general (v. 1b).
   1. Because Christ died for all.
   2. Because Christians care for all.

B. Pray for those in authority in particular (v. 2a).
   1. Those in places of rule and authority.
   2. Those who have influence over our lives.

III. We Have Good Reasons to Pray.

A. The primary reason we should pray (v. 4).
   1. It is God's will for people to be saved (2 Peter 3:9).
   2. It is God's will for all to know the truth.

B. The secondary reason we should pray.
   1. That we might lead peaceable lives (v. 2b).
   2. This is important to the church.
      a. Important to the practice of religion.
      b. Important to the preaching of the gospel.
   3. We are to live in godliness and honesty (v. 2c).
      a. Godliness is our duty toward God.
      b. Honesty is our duty toward human beings.

IV. We Have a Way to Pray (v. 8).

A. We are to pray in holiness (in fellowship with God).

B. We are to pray without wrath (in fellowship with other people).

C. We are to pray without doubting (in fellowship with self).

30

Godliness and Contentment

1 Timothy 6:6

I. **Some Are Godly but Not Content.**
  A. What does this mean?
    1. It means saved but not satisfied.
    2. It means not having joy and peace.
  B. Some reasons for this condition.
    1. Having no real assurance of salvation.
    2. Being carnal in lifestyle.
    3. Not having been taught correctly.
    4. Not understanding victorious living.
    5. Being too lazy to launch out into the deeper life.

II. **Some Are Content but Not Godly.**
  A. How can one be lost and content?
    1. Jesus told about such in Luke 12:13–21.
      a. Some are content because of material fullness.
      b. Some are content because of material security.
    2. Parable of Sower—thorns choked out the Word.
  B. The purpose of the church in the world.
    1. As a witness to the spiritually dead.
    2. The psalmist came to understand (Ps. 73:3–17).

III. **Some Are Neither Godly nor Content.**
  A. Many of the unsaved are not content.
    1. Two areas of human unhappiness.
      a. The outward life or one's circumstances.
      b. The inner life or one's condition of heart.
    2. Solomon had a combination (Ecclesiastes).
  B. The gospel adds to one's discontent as it presses God's claims on us.

IV. **The Ideal Is Godliness and Contentment.**
  A. It is desirable to be saved and satisfied.
    1. This is possible for every person.
    2. Paul had attained this (Phil. 4:11).
  B. Two rules that lead to this.
    1. Believe that God is able.
    2. Believe that God is willing. Study 2 Timothy 4:14–18.

31

What Is a Christian?

2 Timothy 2:15

I. **A Christian Is a Worker.**
  A. This fact is assumed in the text.
    1. We are not told to become workers.
    2. There are no arguments to justify not working.
  B. Every Christian is expected to serve (work).
    1. We are expected to emulate Jesus (John 5:17).
    2. We are saved to serve (Eph. 2:10).
    3. We are called "servants" of God.
    4. We are to be lights (Matt. 5:16).
    5. We are laborers with God (2 Cor. 6:1).
    6. Faith without works is dead (James 2:17).

II. **A Christian Is a Learner.**
  A. This is part of our preparation for work.
    1. What we are to do—"study."
    2. What we are to study—"word of truth."
    3. What we are to learn—"rightly divide."
  B. There are other things profitable to study.
    1. Techniques others have found successful.
    2. Programs which can be helpful.
    3. Principles which have been proven true.
  C. Two things that are inexcusable in a Christian.
    1. Ignorance of the Word of God.
    2. Inactivity in the work of God.

III. **A Christian Is a Seeker.**
  A. We are to seek approval.
    1. We are not to seek man's approval.
    2. We are to seek God's approval.
  B. We are to seek to be approved workers.
    1. The parable of the servants (Luke 19:11–26).
    2. We are to seek to be good stewards.

32
Useless Things

2 Timothy 3:5

There are many useless things in the world. Consider three of the most useless.

I. Religion Without a Savior.
- A. There are several such religions today.
  1. The Hinduism, Moslem, Buddhism, New Age, etc.
  2. Some religions even masquerade as Christianity.
- B. Three reasons it is useless.
  1. It won't get you to heaven.
  2. It won't give you security (peace).
  3. It won't meet your need.
     - a. All are sinners and need a Savior (Rom. 3:23).
     - b. We cannot save ourselves (Titus 3:5).

II. Religion Without a Heart.
- A. A lot of religion is sentimentality.
- B. There is a kind of religion that does not care for others.
  1. Like the priest and Levite had (Luke 10:31–32).
  2. Like the rich man had (Luke 16:19–22).
- C. Three reasons it is useless.
  1. Because it doesn't provide a loving fellowship.
  2. Because it won't involve you in service.
     - a. Saying: "Those who don't care, don't serve; those who don't serve, don't care."
     - b. This mindset may explain why it is so hard to get some people involved.
  3. Because it cannot make you Christ-like (Acts 10:38).

III. Religion Without Stewardship.
- A. Stewardship has to do with responsibility.
  1. Recall the parable of the Good Samaritan (Luke 10).
     - a. The robbers didn't believe in stewardship.

    b. The priest and Levite had religion without stewardship.
    c. The Samaritan was a conscientious steward.
  2. A steward is a trustee—one charged with responsibility.
B. Because it does not build up God's kingdom.
  1. It does not encourage evangelism.
  2. It does not undergird missions.

33
Salvation

Titus 2:11–15

I. **The Origin of Salvation.**
   A. God's love is the origin (John 3:16).
      1. That love is not obtained by good works.
      2. That love was not procured by the Savior's works.
         a. God loved us before Jesus went to the cross.
         b. God's love *sent* Jesus to the cross (Rom. 5:8).
   B. God's grace is the means.
      1. It appeared in the declaration of the angels (Luke 2:11).
      2. It appeared in the revelation of Scripture (1 Peter 1:10).
      3. It appeared in the person of Jesus Christ (John 1:17).
      4. It appeared in the lives of the saints (2 Cor. 3:2).

II. **The Procuring Cause of Salvation (v. 14a).**
   A. Salvation was procured on the cross.
      1. It was purchased by the death of Jesus.
      2. It is the one and only way (John 14:6).
   B. Salvation comes through the work of Jesus (Rom. 10:13–14).
      1. Many try to strike a deal with God.
      2. Many try to find salvation in sacraments.
      3. Many try to find salvation in church membership.
      4. Many try to find salvation in benevolent works.
   C. Salvation can be found only in one place (Acts 4:12).

III. **The Purpose Behind Salvation (vv. 12–14b).**
   A. To fit us for service (Eph. 2:8–10).
   B. To fit us for heaven.
   C. The process by which we are made fit.
      1. There is cleansing from sin (v. 14a).
         a. Zechariah's prophecy (Zech. 13:1).
         b. How much more the blood (Heb. 9:13–14).
      2. There is renewing (v. 14b).

34

The Molder of Lives

Titus 3:3–8

- I. **What We Were in the Past (v. 3).**
  - A. We were disobedient toward God (v. 3a).
    - 1. Sin had dominion over us.
    - 2. Satan had the victory over us.
  - B. We were guilty of sins of the flesh (v. 3b).
    - 1. Such sins are the destroyers of nations.
      - a. These have destroyed great nations of the past.
      - b. Our nation reels from the effect of immorality, substance abuse, etc.
    - 2. Even God's people can be brought down by these sins (remember Samson, David, Noah, etc.).
    - 3. Sins were natural to us before we were saved.
  - C. We were guilty of sins of disposition (v. 3c).
    - 1. These burden the church (pride, envy, etc.).
    - 2. These were normal before we were saved.
- II. **What We Are at the Present (vv. 4–7).**
  - A. We have a heavenly portion (vv. 4–6).
    - 1. We have a love from heaven (v. 4).
    - 2. We have a salvation from heaven (vv. 5, 7a).
    - 3. We have a comforter from heaven (vv. 5b–6).
  - B. We have a heavenly position.
    - 1. We are the heirs of God (v. 7).
    - 2. We are the sons of God.
- III. **What We Need to Be Personally.**
  - A. We need to be personally committed.
    - 1. To God (v. 8a).
    - 2. To do good works (v. 8b; Eph. 2:10).
  - B. We will be personally profited (v. 8c).
    - 1. Now (Eph. 1:3).
    - 2. In the future.

35

The Difference Christ Makes

Philemon 8–16

I. The Difference in the Innocent.

A. Paul was guiltless in this situation.

1. He had not encouraged the slave to run away.
2. He had not tried to conceal the slave.

B. Paul behaved honorably in this situation.

1. Honorably toward the slave, Onesimus.
   a. He persuaded him to do right (v. 12).
   b. He sent a letter in his behalf (v. 10).
2. Honorably toward the master, Philemon.
   a. He would not exercise spiritual authority (vv. 8–9).
   b. He would not keep Onesimus (v. 13).
   c. He would not override Philemon's wishes (v. 14).

C. Christ makes honorable people out of sinners.

II. The Difference in the Guilty.

A. Onesimus had three options.

1. He could refuse to return to Philemon.
2. He could run away from Paul.
3. He could return home to Philemon.

B. The course that Onesimus chose.

1. He was willing to take Paul's counsel (v. 12).
2. He was willing to return to Philemon (v. 15).
3. He was willing to trust his situation to Jesus.

C. Christ makes honest people out of sinners.

III. The Difference in the Victim.

A. Philemon was the victim in this scenario.

B. We are not told what Philemon did.

1. Onesimus was allowed to serve (Col. 4:9).
2. Paul had confidence in his character (v. 14).

C. Jesus Christ does make a difference.

1. He died to reconcile sinners to God (2 Cor. 5:18).
2. He died to reconcile sinners to each other (Eph. 2:14).

D. Christ makes reasonable people out of sinners.

36

The Bible

Hebrews 1:1–2

The Bible is available to all. How are we to profit from the Bible?

I. Have a Right Assessment of the Bible.

- A. What we believe will determine its effect.
  1. Much junk mail is never opened.
  2. Everyone makes judgments about what the Bible is.
- B. There are some things we must accept about the Bible.
  1. It is the Word of God (2 Tim. 3:16; 2 Peter 1:21).
  2. It is the word of life (John 12:28; Matt. 13:18–23).
  3. It is food for the spirit.
     - a. It is called our milk (1 Peter 2:2).
     - b. It is called our honey (Ps. 119:103).
     - c. It is called our meat (Heb. 5:12–14).
  4. It is a guide for life (Ps. 119:105).
  5. It is a weapon for combat (Eph. 6:17).
  6. It is a treasure book (Ps. 19:10).

II. Make a Right Approach to the Bible.

- A. There is a right way to approach the Bible.
  1. We must believe God is going to speak.
  2. We must have an open mind so we can hear God.
- B. There are some rules for approaching the Bible.
  1. The Bible must be read.
  2. The Bible must be believed.
  3. The Bible must be understood.
     - a. We do not need to understand all of theology.
     - b. We do not need to understand every passage.
     - c. The Holy Spirit will guide us (John 14:26).

37
We See Jesus

Hebrews 2:9

Do you see Jesus in your time of need? We see Jesus when . . .

I. We Look for Salvation (John 5:39).
- A. We see Jesus incarnate.
- B. We see Jesus crucified.
  1. It is not enough to see a prophet or a teacher.
  2. We must see Jesus dying for us.
- C. We see Jesus buried and raised again.
- D. We see Jesus interceding for us (1 John 2:1).
- E. We see Jesus coming again.

II. We Look for Strength.
- A. We need strengths of many kinds.
  1. Strength to withstand the attacks of Satan.
  2. Strength to endure sorrow and heartache.
  3. Strength to witness and serve.
- B. We often look for it in the wrong places.
- C. We see Jesus the conqueror.
- D. We see Jesus' Comforter, the indweller.
  1. The Spirit dwells in every believer.
  2. Acts 1:8: "Ye shall receive power after. . . ."

III. We Look for Sustenance.
- A. Israel needed sustenance in the wilderness.
- B. We must learn to trust God.
  1. We worry too much about our needs.
  2. We trust in our own ability to meet our needs.
  3. Jesus urged us to trust God (Matt. 6).
  4. C. H. Spurgeon said: "He will either lighten your burden or he will strengthen your back."

38

If You Have a Need

James 1:5

I. The Need—"If Any Man Lack. . . ."

A. The occasion for this prayer is a need.

1. In this case the need was for wisdom.
2. In your case it may be something else.

B. A need is the only condition set forth.

II. The Method—"Let Him Ask."

A. This approach is not what one would naturally choose. We try man's methods first.

B. Asking is the only method God gives for meeting needs (Phil. 4:6; John 14:13).

III. The Source—"Of God."

A. We go in every direction looking for answers.

B. There is only one source that never fails (Phil. 4:19). A child praying during World War II said, "God bless the President and my parents and, God, take care of yourself 'cause if anything happens to you, we're sunk!"

IV. The Measure—"Giveth to All Liberally."

A. Liberal means "with an open hand."

1. God is not stingy with his blessings.
2. God holds out his hand and says, "Take what you need."

B. Some never find answers to their needs (James 4:2b).

V. The Certainty—"It Shall Be Given Him."

A. People are not *always* willing to give.

B. The word "shall" is an absolute.

1. God is able.
2. God is willing.

39
The Tongue

James 3:1–17

I. The Potential of the Tongue.
- A. It has potential for great good (v. 9a).
  1. We are most noble when we pray.
  2. We are most useful when we witness.
  3. We are most loving when we encourage.
  4. The tongue was meant to glorify God.
- B. It has potential for great harm (v. 9b).
  1. It is a deadly weapon of destruction.
     - a. It has power to defame individuals.
     - b. It has power to divide families.
     - c. It has power to destroy churches.
     - d. It has power to deaden the gospel.
  2. It has the ability to defile.
     - a. It can defile the body (v. 6).
     - b. It can defile the heart (Matt. 12:35).
     - c. It can confuse the life (v. 16).

II. The Power Behind the Tongue.
- A. Nobody controls his/her own tongue (v. 8).
- B. When we are doing good, God is in control (v. 17).
  1. The tongue has been subjected to Christ (1 Cor. 9:27).
  2. Life is to be subjected to Christ (v. 2).
- C. When we do evil things, Satan is in control (vv. 6, 14, 15).
  1. We are servants of the ones we obey (Rom. 6:16).
  2. This is one of Satan's methods of operation (Matt. 12:36–37).

III. The Control of the Tongue.
- A. Get your heart right with God.
  1. The tongue expresses what is in the heart.
  2. If God is to control the tongue, he must rule the heart.
- B. Be quick to reconcile (v. 2).
  1. All of us offend at one time or another.
  2. What you do about the offense is important (Matt. 5:22–24).
  3. Another rule to help in reconciling—confine judgments only to the persons concerned (Matt. 18:15).

40

Reasonable Conduct

1 Peter 1:13–21

I. A Call to Personal Preparedness.

A. Peter called on Christians to guard themselves.

1. To set up a defense against the enemy—self (fifteen personal pronouns are found in text).
2. We are told to "take heed" (1 Tim. 4:16).

B. Three things he told them to do (v. 13).

1. Gird up their minds.
   a. Like a football player puts on his pads.
   b. Paul likened it to a warrior (Eph. 6:14).
   c. The mind is the arena of action.
2. Be sober.
   a. Be alert to spiritual dangers.
   b. Like a boxer who keeps his guard up.
3. Hope to the end.
   a. He warned them against discouragement.
   b. He reminded them of the source of hope—grace.
   c. He reminded them of the method of hope—revelation.
   d. He reminded them of the object of hope—Jesus.

II. A Call to Personal Holiness.

A. He told them to be "obedient" children.

1. This is the "strait" gate and "narrow" way (Matt. 7:14).
2. This involves both negative and positive obedience.

B. Our main business is to be holy.

1. Our first duty is to manage our hearts (Matt. 7:3–5).
2. We are to be holy because God is holy (vv. 15–16).

C. Holiness is a condition for answered prayer (v. 17).

1. Unholiness will hinder our prayers (Ps. 66:18).
2. The God we pray to is also our judge (v. 17).

III. A Call to Personal Assurance.

A. Because of the price that was paid (vv. 18–19).

1. The price was high (Acts 20:28).
2. The price gives us special value to God.
3. The price was agreed on eons ago (v. 20).

B. We should not think lightly of our salvation.

41

War Against the Church

1 Peter 5:8

I. **Some Weapons Satan Uses (2 Cor. 2:11).**
   A. Weapon #1—loose tongues.
      1. World War II motto: "Loose lips sink ships."
      2. James 3:6 identifies the weapon.
      3. Matthew 7:1 tells us not to judge.
   B. Weapon #2—discouraged workers.
      1. Two tactics he uses against workers.
         a. He discourages some from serving.
         b. He disheartens some who are serving.
      2. He will throw obstacles in our path.
      3. We need encouragement (1 Cor. 15:58; Gal. 6:9).
   C. Weapon #3—stirred-up emotions.
      1. Emotions are like dynamite.
         a. It doesn't take much to set them off.
         b. They can do a lot of damage.
      2. Satan concentrates on your Achilles' heel.
   D. Weapon #4—conflict and confusion over issues.
      1. Satan is a master at twisting things.
         a. In Eden he twisted the word of God.
         b. He can twist the truth and make it seem a lie.
         c. He can twist a lie and make it seem the truth.
      2. Satan must be recognized in all church conflicts.

II. **Some Defenses for Satan's Weapons.**
   A. Defense #1—be alert and watchful.
      1. We must be aware of what is happening.
      2. We must speak spiritually not carnally.
   B. Defense #2—put up some resistance.
      1. Commit your tongue to the lordship of Jesus.
      2. Don't let yourself become discouraged (1 Cor. 4:5).
      3. Treat your emotions with respect.

   a. Old saying: "When angry, count to ten."
   b. Keep the dynamite "defused."
4. Deal with confusion and conflict reasonably.
   a. Be sure you have all of the facts.
   b. Be aware of other sources of the conflict.
   c. Love one another (1 John 3:23).

42

Life's Most Important Decision

2 Peter 1:3–4

Recount many important decisions people make. The most important decision is to receive Jesus as Savior. Why is this decision so important?

I. It Settles the Sin Problems.

- A. Everyone has two sin problems.
  1. The problem of sin's consequences.
     - a. The wages of sin (Rom. 6:23).
     - b. The lake of fire (Rev. 20:15).
     - c. When one accepts Jesus, this problem is resolved.
  2. The problem of sin's power.
     - a. All fail in their own efforts not to sin.
     - b. There is an answer to overcoming sin.
       - (1) Sin is a law (Rom. 7:21).
       - (2) Human strength cannot overcome a law.
       - (3) Only a stronger law can overcome a law.
       - (4) There is a stronger law (Rom. 8:2).
- B. Everyone needs Jesus for this reason.

II. It Settles the Destiny Question.

- A. Everyone must spend eternity someplace.
  1. The Bible says there are only two places.
  2. Every person has an option regarding eternity.
- B. Sign often seen: "Where will you spend eternity?"

III. It Settles the Authority Challenge.

- A. Every life has an authority crisis.
  1. Satan wants to be lord of our lives.
  2. Jesus wants to be lord of our lives.
- B. When we accept Jesus it is settled.

43

Remaining Lost Is Hard Work

2 Peter 3:9

God works hard to save sinners. Sinners must work hard to remain lost.

I. **They Must Resist the Efforts of the Church.**
   A. The church is sent to call sinners to salvation.
   B. Sinners are the target of the church's action.
      1. Like Jonah, they must run (Jonah 1:3).
      2. Like David, they are confronted (2 Sam. 12:7).

II. **They Must Renounce the Words of the Bible.**
   A. The Bible says we all need to be saved.
   B. The Bible says Jesus is the only way (John 14:6).
   C. The Bible says everyone may come (Rev. 22:17).
      1. A sinner must work hard to escape.
      2. The Bible will accuse him in the day of judgment.

III. **They Must Repress Their Own Conscience.**
   A. A man had a bell over the door of his store to warn him.
   B. God put consciences in people to warn them.
      1. Our conscience appeals to our better judgment.
      2. A sinner must agonize to get past his conscience.

IV. **They Must Retreat from Family and Friends.**
   A. Many loved ones long and pray for their salvation.
   B. Some try to share Jesus with them.
   C. A sinner must retreat from concerned Christians to remain lost.

V. **They Must Resist the Holy Spirit.**
   A. The Spirit stands between the sinner and hell.
      1. Recall Balaam's vision (Num. 22:21–31).
      2. The Pharisees resisted (Acts 7:51).
   B. The sinner must get past this roadblock.

VI. They Must Reject the Son of God.

A. Hear the words of the Savior from Calvary (Isa. 1:18; John 3:36; Matt. 11:28).

B. One must trample underfoot the Son of God (Heb. 10:29).

44
The Effects of Sin

1 John 2:1

John was concerned about Christians sinning. Other disciples were equally concerned. James said it brings forth death (James 1:15). Paul said not to let it reign (Rom. 6:12). The disciples had good reason for concern.

I. Sin Affects Our Relationship to God.
- A. It affects God's feelings and actions toward us.
  1. Our fellowship is affected (1 John 1:7).
  2. Sin is a bottleneck to God's blessings.
- B. It affects our feelings about God.
  1. It steals our affection away (Matt. 6:24).
  2. It deadens our interest in the things of God.
     - a. It will kill prayer life.
     - b. It will destroy witness.
     - c. It will stifle good stewardship.
     - d. It will interfere with Bible study.
     - e. It will hinder church involvement.
     - f. It will make service ineffectual.

II. Sin Affects Our Relationship to People.
- A. It affects our relationship to the saved.
  1. It quenches the Spirit, our bond of unity.
  2. It neutralizes our love for God's people.
  3. It destroys the joy of salvation (Ps. 51:12).
- B. It affects our relationship to family and friends.
  1. It is the cause of family conflicts.
  2. It is the destroyer of friendships.
- C. It affects our relationship to the unsaved.
  1. A Christian should be two things to the unsaved.
     - a. A light to show the way (Matt. 5:16).
     - b. A voice to warn of judgment (Ezek. 33:8).
  2. Sin puts out the light and stills the voice.
- D. It must be dealt with daily (1 John 1:9).

45

What Makes You So Special?

1 John 4:21

We don't always treat each other well. We don't have a sense of the worth of others. Jesus referred to human worth (Mark 8:36–37). We don't always treat ourselves very well. We don't have a sense of self-worth. We are very special in God's sight.

I. Because We Are Created in His Image (Gen. 1:26).

A. Every person has an innate worth.
  1. Not based on conduct or lifestyle.
  2. Based on origin—created in God's image.

B. We have worth because of *who* not *what* we are.
  1. Creatures formed for a special position.
  2. Creatures formed for a special purpose.

II. Because Christ Died for Us (Heb. 2:9).

A. The Bible tells us why Jesus died.
  1. Not because he could not prevent it.
  2. It was necessary for our redemption.

B. The Bible tells us who Jesus died for.
  1. John 3:16—the world: whosoever believeth.
  2. This includes every one of us and gives each one value.

C. God has made a great investment in us.
  1. He invested his only begotten Son.
  2. The amount of investment determines value.

III. Because God Is No Respecter of Persons (Acts 10:34).

A. God doesn't show favoritism (2 Peter 3:9).

B. What should this mean to us?
  1. We should open our hearts to all people.
  2. We should consider ourselves of value.

46

Greatness in Twos

2 John 4–11

I. **Two Great Commandments.**
   A. Command to walk in truth (v. 4).
      1. This is the essence of the Christian religion.
      2. Two possible meanings of this.
         a. Live a life of honesty and integrity.
         b. Live according to true biblical tenets.
      3. The world judges Christians by this.
   B. Command to walk in love (v. 5).
      1. This is the foundation of the Christian religion.
      2. This is the badge of discipleship (John 13:35).
         a. Soldiers are known by their uniforms.
         b. Jews were known by their external rites.
         c. Christians are known by their love for one another.
      3. This is evidence of our love for Jesus (Matt. 25:40; John 14:21).
      4. This is necessary for the well-being of the church.

II. **Two Great Doctrines.**
   A. Doctrine of Christ in the flesh (v. 7).
      1. This is a basic doctrine of the Christian religion.
         a. It has to do with the incarnation.
            (1) Some said he only "appeared" to be a man.
            (2) This would negate part of the atonement.
         b. It identifies Jesus with humanity.
      2. Important related passages: John 19:34–35; John 20:26–27; 1 John 5:6.
   B. Doctrine of Christ (v. 9).
      1. Two possible meanings of this.
         a. Teachings about Christ.
         b. Teachings of Christ.
      2. One must believe certain things about Christ (Rom. 10:9; 1 John 4:2–3).
      3. One must live by the teachings of Jesus (John 8:12).
      4. Notice the walk that pleases God (Col. 1:10).

47

What About Missions?

3 John 5–11

I. **Paul Commended the Support of Missions.**
    A. Four things Paul called this support.
        1. He called it being faithful (v. 5).
        2. He called it doing well (v. 6).
        3. He called it doing right (v. 8).
        4. He called it good (v. 11).
    B. Two ways one may support missions.
        1. One may go as a missionary.
            a. Evidently some had done that (v. 5).
            b. Paul commended these people for two things.
                (1) For going out for the sake of Jesus (v. 7a).
                (2) For not taking money from believers (v. 7b).
            c. Many serve as missionaries today.
        2. One may provide for those who do go.
            a. Every little bit is commendable (v. 5).
            b. Support of missionaries does two things.
                (1) Brings them forward on their journey (v. 6).
                (2) Makes us fellow helpers in their mission (v. 8).
    C. Every church should be involved in missions.

II. **Paul Condemned Opposition to Missions.**
    A. Missionaries carried letters of recommendation.
        1. Paul had written such letters (v. 9a).
        2. Diotrephes opposed missions in three ways.
            a. He disregarded Paul's recommendation (v. 9b).
            b. He would not receive the missionaries (v. 10b).
            c. He would not allow others to support them (v. 10c).
    B. Some Christians do not support missions today.
        1. Some disregard the call of God.
        2. Some refuse to provide for those who do go.
        3. Some actively oppose church support of missions.
    C. Paul made two comparisons (v. 11).
        1. A comparison between good and evil.
        2. A comparison between being of God or not.
        3. Attitude toward missions was the deciding factor.

48

Duties

Jude 17–24

I. The Christian's Duties (vv. 20–23).

A. To build yourself up (v. 20).
   1. Build according to a system based on faith.
   2. Build on a foundation already laid (Eph. 2:20).

B. To pray in the Holy Ghost (v. 20).
   1. It is our duty to pray (Eph. 6:18).
   2. It is necessary to pray in the Spirit (Rom. 8:26–27).

C. To keep yourself in the love of God (v. 21).
   1. Keep yourself in love *with* God (John 15:9).
   2. Staying in love requires some effort.

D. To look for mercy unto eternal life (v. 21).
   1. This means to look for his coming (Titus 2:13).
      a. To look is to believe he is coming.
      b. To look is to be ready for his coming.
   2. This coming is the fulfillment of his mercy.

E. To be involved in evangelism (vv. 22–23).
   1. This is every Christian's responsibility (Matt. 28:18–20).
   2. There are two ways to evangelize.
      a. With tenderness and meekness (v. 22).
      b. With the threat of future judgment (v. 23a).
   3. There is a danger in evangelizing (v. 23b).
      a. The danger of being adversely influenced.
      b. We must love sinners but hate sin.

II. The Savior's Duties (v. 24).

A. To keep you from falling.
   1. There are two ways Christians can fall (see v. 4).
      a. In lifestyle.
      b. In beliefs.
   2. The Savior is able to keep us from stumbling.
   3. We have a duty to those who do fall (Gal. 6:1–2).

B. To present you faultless before God.
   1. He does this through his death (Col. 1:22).
   2. He does this through his Spirit (John 14:26; 16:13).
   3. It will be a time of exceeding joy.

49

What Every Person Needs to Do

Revelation 3:20

Consider three things every person needs to do.

I. We Need to Consider—God Has.
- A. God has considered our situation.
  1. Most Christians believe that God sees our wrongs (Jer. 13:27).
  2. We must believe that God also sees our need.
     - a. Our need for a Savior (John 3:16).
     - b. Our need for a light (1 Peter 2:9).
- B. We also need to consider our situation.
  1. The psalmist thought on his ways (Ps. 119:59).
  2. We must see what God has seen.
     - a. Adam and Eve considered (Gen. 3:7, 21).
     - b. We must see ourselves as sinners in need.
     - c. We must see Jesus as the answer to our need.

II. We Need to Decide—God Has.
- A. Notice some things God has already decided.
  1. That he doesn't want anyone to perish (2 Peter 3:9).
  2. That those who believe in Jesus will not perish (John 3:18).
  3. That if we will open the door, he will come in.
- B. We also need to decide some things.
  1. That we do not want to perish.
     - a. Jonah was unconcerned about his situation (Jon. 1:5).
     - b. Many today are unconcerned about their situation.
     - c. This is why the church must be concerned.
  2. That we will put our trust in Jesus (1 John 5:12).
  3. That we will open the door.

III. We Need to Act—God Has.
- A. God has already acted in our behalf.
  1. God gave his Son for our sins (John 3:16).

2. God gave his Word to guide us to salvation (John 20:31).
3. God gave the church to call us to salvation.

B. We must act on our own behalf.
1. We need to decide to trust Jesus.
2. We need to confess that decision openly.

50

The Gospel Call

Revelation 14:6–7

I. "Fear God" Refers to the Sinner's Need.

A. The lost person does not fear God.

1. "Fear" means have reverence for God.
2. The unsaved are in rebellion against God.

B. The gospel calls us to "fear God."

1. This is part of the salvation experience.
2. This is part of the reconciliation experience.

II. "Give Glory" Refers to the Christian Life.

A. It is impossible for the unsaved to glorify God.

B. It is possible for the saved not to glorify God.

1. When they do not follow God's will.
2. When they do not obey God's Word.

C. God is glorified when we walk in fellowship.

1. When we walk in fellowship with God.
2. When we walk in fellowship with each other.

III. "Judgment" Refers to Our Meeting with God.

A. Every person has an unavoidable appointment.

1. "It is appointed unto men . . ." (Heb. 9:27).
2. This appointment has been set up by God.

B. Everyone will have to give an accounting.

1. "Everyone must give account . . ." (Rom. 14:12).
2. It will be terrible for the unsaved (Rev. 6:16).
3. It will be joyous for the saved (Matt. 25:34).

IV. "Worship" Refers to the Life Beyond.

A. God has declared that we should worship Jesus (Phil. 2:10).

1. It will be the Christian's pleasure.
2. It will be the punishment of the unsaved.
3. It will not be anyone's prerogative.

B. The gospel calls us to worship.